Contents

© 1987 by Faber Music Ltd
First published in 1987 by Faber Music Ltd
3 Queen Square London WC1N 3AU
Music drawn by Lincoln Castle Music
Cover illustration by Penny Dann
Cover design by M & S Tucker
Printed in England by Caligraving Ltd

Violin part, cello part and piano score are sold separately.

1. Open String Samba

Stringpops 1

fun pieces for absolute beginners

VIOLIN/CELLO & PIANO

Peter Wilson

String parts edited by Madeleine Ranger

Faber Music Limited
London

Preface

Learning an instrument should be enjoyable. If children are bored they will be much less willing to assimilate new ideas and techniques, and progress will be slow – dull practice routines can stunt musical development!

But while there's plenty of material in a 'serious' vein for beginner violinists and cellists, little attempt has been made to use popular musical idioms in teaching contexts. This is a missed opportunity. Because it is so widely available and so readily understood, it is often popular music that provides children with their earliest musical stimulus, and a real need exists for popular material with educational value.

This is what we have set out to provide in *Stringpops*. Each piece has its place in a carefully planned progression that takes the learner violinist or cellist through the fundamentals of string technique, starting with the simplest open string patterns and continuing in first position. The series is designed to be suitable for both class and individual teaching, and the violin and cello parts can stand on their own or be combined as a duo. The music has been well tested in many schools within the Tower Hamlets String Project of the Inner London Education Authority, with exciting and encouraging results.

Technical and musical features introduced in Book 1 include the following: open string crossing at different speeds (*Open String Samba*); accentuation (*Calypso*); dynamic contrasts, tremolo (*March of the Cadets*); first position (all fingers), rest-counting (*Bow Rock*); short and long bows, *crescendo* and *diminuendo* (*Piccadilly Ballad*); new finger-positions for F and C natural, *pizzicato* (*Jazz Waltz*); lifted up-bow (ie ♩· ♩), double-stopping on open strings (*Sky Diver*).

We would like to thank Penny Dann for the lively illustrations she has provided for the violin and cello parts. Pupils can be encouraged to colour these in after learning the appropriate piece.

Peter Wilson

Madeleine Ranger

2. Calypso

3. March of the Cadets

8

con 8va bassa ad lib.

4. Bow Rock

Go for it! (♩ = 132)

f marcato

f marcato

f marcato

f

con 8va bassa ad lib.

5. Piccadilly Ballad

2nd time to CODA

14

6. Jazz Waltz

7. Sky Diver